AVYAYA P R

Avyaya P R is a 10 year old school going young girl. Avyaya's mother's name is Binumol Shaji & father's name is Rilsin.P.R. Avyaya is currently residing in the United Kingdom. She was born in Kochi.

She has done her primary schooling in St. Arnold's Central School, Aduvassery, Kochi & Chinmaya Vidyalaya, Cannanore. She is active in studies & has participated in many Co-curricular school activities. She is an active participant of International Maths, English, Social studies & Science Olympiad. Last year she attained 2nd rank in school level for English Olympiad & 1st rank for Maths Olympiad. Her Maths Olympiad score was ranked 6th Internationally bringing laurels to the school. She loves adventure sports & travelling. She also loves writing in her leisure time & this is her first book as an author.

English Language
Magical Wand
(Children's Literature)
by
Avyaya

Published in July 2022
by Kairali Books Private Limited
Thalikkavu Road, Kannur.
Ph : 0497-2761200
E-Mail : kairalibooksknr@gmail.com

Illustrations
Smitha K.E.

Cover Design & Layout
Prasanth Mangad

Price : 180.00
16/22-23/Sl.No.1321/POD 250/NS 18.6
ISBN 978-93-93397-00-3

Magical Wand

Avyaya

Kairali Books

Dedication

This book is dedicated to
my aunt Anumol and Ammunni
who inspired me to read books.
Also to my Achuttan who buys me books
since I was a 3year old.

Contents

Chapter 1

How did they find the Magical Wand

Once upon a time there lived three children Cole, Ruby and Molly. They are going to a mysterious place called Savannah with their parents. They went to the Airport and boarded the flight. It was a very big plane. Finally, they reached their new home in Savannah at night. And they went to sleep.... In the morning the sky was blue as blueberries. They had their breakfast.

Mother: Children you have to do some chores today. Paint and decorate the garage. The paint and things to decorate are kept in the attic.

Ruby: Will you help us mother???

Mother: Sorry Ruby. Me and your father are going to an interview to get a Job.

Molly: Ok. All the best Mom.

Their parents went to attend their interviews.

Cole: Let's go to the attic.

They found paint and decor items there.

Molly: Wait a minute I saw a box like a chest!!!! I mean treasure chest!!!!!! Let's Go open it.

When they opened the chest....

The Children: Omg

They found a crystal ball, a sheet of folded paper and a wand.

Cole: I wonder where mother and father are now??? I wish they could be here too.

As quick as lightning a puff of smoke came out of the crystal ball.

Ruby: Omg we can see mother and father inside the crystal ball!!!! Let's open the paper.

Written on the paper

Hi!

You are lucky to live here. I will tell you how the Magical wand works. (When the wand glows, shake it three times and it will take you to a dreadful place or an amazing

Smitha

Smitha

place.)

Cole: Next it is showing how to use the crystal ball. We already know that the crystal ball shows the whereabouts of the people we ask for.

Ruby: Well, the wand is not glowing now. So, let's paint and decorate the garage. I am not going to tell mother and father about the wand & the crystal ball now. I guess they will not allow us to use it.

Cole and Molly: Yeah, we will also not tell them now.

Ruby: I'll paint the garage door baby blue.

Cole: Well, I'm going to decorate the garage with artificial flowers and more. I will also paint the upper part of the garage cerulean blue.

Molly: I am going to paint the walls of the garage ultramarine blue.

They painted and decorated the garage very beautifully and even their parents were astonished and happy to see their work.

Chapter 2

Village of Candy

Two days later...

Cole: Girls! Come on let's check the magical wand.

Molly: Ok.

The Children: Omg.

Cole: The Magical Wand is glowing!!! Let's shake it three times.

Ruby: I hope it will take us to an Amazing land!! Let's also take our crystal ball along.

Molly shook the wand three times.

As quick as lightning, pink sparkles came out of the wand and they all went into the wand.

Smitha

The Children : Awesome

Molly: I guess we reached an amazing place. I wonder where we are??? As quick as lightning, a puff of smoke came out of the crystal ball. It showed that they were in the Village of candy!!!!!

Ruby: Is it a dream or what!!! All the bushes are made of Marshmallows, Gummy Bears and Bubble Gums here.

Cole: And look! Chewing Gums and Toffees are hanging on the trees!! And Candy Canes are hanging on the plants!! This land is so colorful and bright!!

Molly: Goodies on trees, plants and bushes I have never ever seen in my life!!!!!

Cole: I'm going to pluck Marshmallows and Bubble Gums.

Molly: Well, I'm going to pluck Candy Canes and Gummy Bears.

Ruby: I'm going to pluck ummm Toffees and Chewing Gums.

The Children: yum!!!!!!!

Cole: Who is that coming towards us!!!!!!!! Well he/she looks funny though.

Molly: yeah

Ruby: I don't think he/she looks dangerous

Smitha

at all!

Can you guess who is it!!???

Chapter 3

The Candy Man and how did they find the wormhole ?

The person coming towards the children looked strange.

Molly: Woah her/his body is full of candies!!

Candy Man: Hi there!!

The Children: Uhhhh Hi!

Ruby: Are you a male or a female???

Candy Man: Male of course!! Many people ask me this question I don't know why. You children don't look like the people of the Village of Candy. Where do you come from and what are your names?

Ruby: My name is Ruby and these two are my siblings. His name is Cole and her name is Molly. We are coming from Savannah.

Candy Man: Okay... By the way how did you reach here!!

Cole narrated the whole story to the Candy Man.

Candy Man: Alright children. Can I show you some exciting things to do in the Village of Candy!!!

Cole: Of Course!!

Candy Man: Let's go to the playground!!

The slide is made of very long and wide stripes of chewing gum.

There is a trampoline made of squishy and bouncy toffee.

The children played on the playground. They were tired so they sat on a chair made out of bubble gum and armrest was made of candy canes.

Candy Man: Let's watch a movie at my home!!!!!!

The Children got excited.

The Children: Woohoo!!!! Yay!!!!

Smitha

Candy Man along with the three children walked through the streets of the Village of Candy and reached the Candy Man's house.

It was a beautiful house decorated with daisies, roses, Sweet Williams, lily and many more!!!!!!!

They reached the movie room in the house!!!!!!!

The Sofa was made out of Marshmallows.

The kids enjoyed having gummy bears while watching the movie.

2 hours later.....................

Ruby: That was such a good movie!!!

The Candy Man, Cole and Molly: Yeah, true the movie was indeed very good.

Then they all had a fun chat.

Candy Man: It is getting dark outside. Do you want to go home??

The Children: Yes

Candy Man: I know all about this wand. The places you go using this wand will have a wormhole which you have to find. Once you find it, jump through it and you'll reach home.

Cole: OH... It would be difficult for us to find the wormhole as it is getting dark.

Ruby: Well, I think I saw a hole near to the marshmallow bush in the park. Well, I'm not sure though

Molly: Mother and Father will be mad at us I think, Well, let's go to the park and see if the wormhole is there.

The Children: Bye Candy Man

Candy Man: Bye children. Hope you find the wormhole in the park.

They ran to the park and they found the wormhole near to a marshmallow bush as Ruby said.

Without wasting anytime, they jumped through the hole and reached at the attic in their home.

Ruby: It's 7pm already!! But luckily, Mother and Father are not here yet.

Molly and Cole: Good Gracious!!!

Chapter 4

The Candy Man visited us!!!!

A week passed. The children were busy with their school and home works...

Father: Children, me and your mother are going to work!!

The Children: Ok Bye Father and Mother.

After a while...

At the door: Knock Knock!!!!!

Ruby: Someone's at the door. Let's go & open the door.

They opened the door.

The children: ARE YO-U TH-E CAN-DY MA-N!!!!!!!!!!

Candy Man: Geez!!!!!!! No need to shout!!!!

Cole: How did you come here!!!!! Did someone see you!!!! How did you know that we live here!!! Goodness Sake!!!!!! If Mother and Father were here, they would have been mad at us!!!!!

Molly: Shut up Cole!!!! you're asking too many questions!! Sorry about that Candy Man.

Cole and Ruby: Yeah sorry

Cole: Come in Candy Man.

Molly: Have you had breakfast, Candy man?

Candy Man: Yep but I haven't drunk anything since yesterday.

Ruby: Oh dear!! We have nothing except some hot chocolate, would you like some?

Candy Man: If you won't mind, I would love to!!!!!

Cole: Great!!!

They all had a chat sipping their delicious hot chocolate.

Cole: Candy Man, tell us how did you come here!!!

Candy Man: Well, when I woke up in the

Smitha

Smitha

morning today and went for a walk, I saw the wormhole near to the marshmallow bush in the park. It was very strange. I knew that it is the magical wand's wormhole. I had read the book named "Magical Wand's mystery" that tells everything about the magical wand.

Written in the book about the wormhole:

"If the last person who visited the land, used the wormhole to get back to their home, and You jump through it, you will reach the front door of their house."

More about wormhole was written on page no 406 in that book. It says:

"The wormhole will stay there for years and years.

Sometimes, it will stay there for only 1 hour and 30 minutes and disappear."

Candy Man: This is how I reached here. By the way, is the magical wand glowing now?

Ruby: UMMMM...... UHHHH........ We didn't check. We were busy with our homework.

Candy Man: Well let's go and check and where it is?

Cole: In the attic.

They all went to the attic.

Molly: Look, it's glowing!!!!!!! Let's take the

crystal ball along with us.

Candy Man: Here we go!!!!!!!

Cole shook the wand three times.

As quick as lightning, pink sparkles came out of the wand and they all went into the wand. WHOOSH!!!!!!

Chapter 5

Mr. Daniel Slime

They all reached a new land. The children were wondering whether this land would be an amazing land or a dreadful one.

Children: EWWW!!!!! WHAT IN THE WORLD IS THAT SQUISHY THING!!!!!

Cole: OMG!!!! Did you guys forget about the Crystal ball we have!

Molly: Oh.... Yeah. Let's check.

Molly asked the Crystal ball: I wonder where we are!

As quick as lightning, a puff of smoke came out of the ball.

Candy Man: It's the village of Slime!!!! Here lives a great friend of mine!! But I don't know where does he live exactly.

Ruby: Well, UMMMM It's quite nice. I like squishy thingies.

The Children: OMG!! Look!! There is a Slime Mountain!!!!

Candy Man: TH- THIS IS THE PLACE WERE HE LI- LIVE!!!!!!!!!! He is also a magician!!!!!! Let's climb on the Mountain!!!!!!

They climbed the Mountain. There was a house made with Kinetic Sand, it is almost like slime!!!!!!!

Ruby: Is it your friend's house Candy Man!!!!

Candy Man: UMMM I don't know?? Let's go and check.

There was a bell made with slime hanging outside the house.

Cole rang the bell.

Someone opened the door.

Candy Man: OMG!!!! Mr. Daniel slime!!!!

Mr. Daniel slime: YOU'RE CAN-DY MA-N!!!!!!! Where have you been all these days??

Smitha

Mr. Daniel slime: There are three kids with you!! Who are they??

Cole: I'm Cole

Ruby: I'm Ruby

Molly: Last but not the Least I'm Molly.

Mr. Daniel slime: Well you guys are friendly! Come in guys!!

The Children and the Candy Man: Wow

Candy Man: You decorated your house very well!!!! Super Cool!!

Chapter 6

Exploring the Village of Slime

Mr. Daniel Slime: I'll take something special to eat!!

Cole: Okay

Mr. Daniel Slime said: F-o-o-d-r-i-o.

Some delicious food items appeared suddenly.

Ruby: What an amazing sight!! There came two Goodies. It looked so tasty!

Ruby: What are these Mr. Daniel Slime.

Mr. Daniel Slime: This one is Burst Cupcakes

TOYS
Smitha

Smitha

and that one is Chrome Cookies!!

Molly and Candy Man took one Chrome Cookies each and had a bite. The cookie was topped with almonds and sprinkles were stuffed inside the cookie. It was delicious!!

Cole and Ruby took one Burst Cupcakes each and when they took a bite, caramel sauce came flowing from it. It was so delicious than the Chrome Cookies.

Mr. Daniel Slime: Let's go to Stretchy Toy Centre!

Cole: Well, that sounds interesting!!

Ruby: Well, what are we waiting for? Let's go!!!!

Molly: Wait a second! What kind of toys are there in the Toy Centre?

Mr. Daniel Slime: UMM... There are putties, slimes, kinetic sand, squishies and toys made from putties and slimes.

Ruby: I will buy Slimes.

Molly: I will buy Putties.

Cole: I will umm... buy toys made from Putties for Ruby, Molly and Mother.

Candy Man: I love Squishies so, I will buy Squishes.

Mr. Daniel Slime: I often visit this Toy Centre. I have bought most things from there so, I don't know what to buy.

Cole: Oh, ok can we go now I am so excited!!

Mr. Daniel Slime: Of course, let's go!

They went outside the house and walked...

They reached the Squishy Street...

Mr. Daniel Slime: Here we are at the Toy Centre!! Let's go inside!!!!

Everyone was searching the things they wanted to buy!!

Ruby: OMG!!! CRUNCHY, CLOUDY AND GLITTERY UNICORN SLIME!!!!! THIS IS THE SLIME I WANTED FOR AGES!!!

Molly: OMG!!!! PUTTY THAT CHANGES BLUE TO PURPLE AND GLOWS IN WATER BEST DAY OF MY WHOLE LIFE!!!

Cole: OMG!! CLIPS FOR MOTHER, RUBY AND MOLLY WHICH BECOMES TRANSPARENT AT NIGHT!!!!

Candy Man: SQUISHY THAT CHANGES LIGHT PINK TO HOT PINK WHEN DIPPED IN WATER AND HAS A STRONG BUBBLE GUM SCENT.

Mr. Daniel Slime: Let's go to the check out and pay!

They walked to Mr. Daniel Slime's house.

Mr. Daniel Slime: Guys, if you want you can stay at my house.

Candy Man: If you don't mind, I would love to.

Cole: We would love to, but our parents would certainly be worried.

Ruby: Oh, but there is the wormhole.

Children: Let's go.

Mr. Daniel Slime and Candy Man: It was really good meeting you three. Hope we'll meet soon, bye.

Children: Same, bye.

The children jumped through the hole and reached their house.

Molly: What!! it is so bright outside.

Cole: Well, we're not in the magical land.

Ruby: So, Mother and Father did not come.

Everyone: Good Gracious!!!